FABULOUS WOOL FELT

Stitch 17 Fun Gifts and Projects

SUZANNE COSMO

Published by:
Kansas City Star Books
1729 Grand Blvd.
Kansas City, Missouri, USA 64108

First edition, first printing
ISBN: 978-1-61169-131-3

Library of Congress Control Number:
2014939775

Printed in the United States of America
by Walsworth Publishing Co., Marceline,
MO

To order copies, call StarInfo at
(816) 234-4473.

KansasCityStarQuilts.com

FABULOUS WOOL FELT

Stitch 17 Fun Gifts and Projects

SUZANNE COSMO

Editor: Edie McGinnis

Designer: Kim Walsh

Photography: Aaron T. Leimkuehler

Illustration: Eric Sears

Technical Editor: Jane Miller

Photo Editor: Jo Ann Groves

We are especially grateful to Jan Jabara, owner
of The Hatchery House Bed & Breakfast, for al-
lowing us to use her lovely inn located in historic
Weston, Missouri, for photography.

For more information, visit www.hatcherybb.com.
Or stop by or call
The Hatchery House Bed and Breakfast
618 Short St.
Weston, Missouri 64098
816-640-5700

About the Author

SUZANNE COSMO has been a quilter for more than 30 years and has a lifetime of experience in the fiber and fabric world. She grew up in California where her mother encouraged her and her sisters to explore and collect anything they could find on the beach to make sea/sand gardens. She has brought that creativity to her weaving and her quilts and now brings the freedom of expression to her wool appliqué pieces.

She has taught classes on original, as well as traditional, quilt design. Suzanne's quilts have won many awards and have appeared in national quilt magazines, The Victoria and Albert Museum in the UK and in her one woman show, A Stitch in Time, Rush Haven Coffee Spot and Art Gallery in California.

Suzanne is vice president of her local guild and continues to create art quilts incorporating felt, yarn, beads and fabric.

Her favorite saying:

"Your most creative moment might be today!"

Acknowledgements

I want to thank my husband Greg, a wonderful man who has exhibited patience beyond belief throughout the years of my many projects and interests.

Thanks go to my wonderful daughters: Heather Williams, for putting up with every idea I ever had, and who strongly encouraged me to write this book, and Sally Cosmo for always giving me honest feedback on my work. They are my strength and inspiration.

I want to thank my mom, Coralie Woods. She taught me to sew and to cut straight. She really wanted me to be a secretary, but found out she would rather have a fiber artist for a daughter because it made me happier. We know how moms want their kids to be happy.

Thanks to my sister Helen Eastman, who saw me as an artist from the time we were little girls. She encouraged me at every turn and fed my habit by buying paper, pencils, paint, wool, clay, yarn, glue and fabric for me. She knew I would find the right outlet for the artist inside of me.

Sharon Short, Irene Walker, Rachel Clark, Daren Whitehorn, Kathy Fey, Lisa Egan, Susan Burdick, R'chelle Price Christiansen, Carolynn Stoops, Lenore Meyers and Susan Zerbe, I thank each you for believing in me, making me laugh and giving me advice. You were there on the days when a kind word was just what I needed.

A big thanks to Aaron Leimkuehler for the amazing photography and to Kim Walsh for making the pages looks so lovely. Jane Miller rose to the challenge of doing the technical editing, making sure everything is the right size and there is enough material to make each project happen. A special thanks to my editor, Edie McGinnis, who told me to "just do it." She was there for every question by phone or Facebook. Thank you for your patience, encouragement and support. Thanks also to Doug Weaver, publisher of Kansas City Star Quilts, for the wonderful opportunity to publish this book.

FABULOUS WOOL FELT

Table of Contents

Introduction

I have been creating with fabric, wool, yarn, clay and paint my whole life. My two older sisters and my mother are very creative knitters. They have often tried to get me to knit with them and, although I love the look of yarns and wool and have done some spinning and weaving, I never found the spark of interest they had for knitting. I was drawn to fabric and felt.

We spent many a summer in Mexico as my father saw himself as the old man of the sea and did a great deal of deep sea fishing. On our frequent trips to the local town, I became intrigued with the bright embroidered and appliquéd skirts and tops. My mother bought me one of the skirts, and I wore it all the time, even when I got home to the chagrin of my family.

I grew up and married my husband, Greg. We, like most young couples, were on a budget and had two girls to entertain. Instead of racing off to purchase toys, we often used what we had on hand. We once took the legs off an unused couch and, with a bit of paint and a tuft of wool roving for hair, we turned them into dolls.

After years of working in hospitals and doctors offices, I decided to change my life and go to clown school. Yes, I did. I spent 14 years clowning around. I made my own costumes, to which I added bright appliquéd designs, much like the ones I had seen in Mexico when I was young.

I was hooked on appliqué, so much so that I changed my quilting style from patchwork to appliqué. I took a wool appliqué class and fell in love with it.

Wool appliqué is easily accomplished with few specialty tools. We are able

to buy wool felt at our local fabric store or order it online. We can embrace that simplicity again, and this book will get you started.

I am delighted to introduce you to my designs and to the practical and economical "no-nonsense" world of wool appliqué

There will be no long lecture on felting your own wool, or trudging through thrift stores to find old wool and over dyeing it, a messy, time-consuming process indeed. I operate on the theory that until a sheep shows up on my doorstep asking to be shorn, I will just buy my wool and have a great time.

There are so many colors of wool to choose from and, by adding traditional or whimsical embroidery and embellishments, your design possibilities are endless. I am here to encourage you to try this technique and make delightful additions to your home or fun gifts for your friends and family.

Enjoy!
Suzanne.

General Instructions

Read all instructions first.

I recommend that you wash and dry all the felt or felted wool that comes into your home or workshop. Give it a light press, and you are ready for your project.

Choose a project. Trace the pattern from the book onto the dull side of freezer paper. Decide on the colors you want for each element of your design. Cut it into squares a bit larger than each pattern piece and iron onto your felt pieces, shiny side down.

On larger pieces of the project, measurements are given and pieces can be cut without using freezer paper.

Cut out all the elements of the design.

Lay out all the design elements onto the top layer of felt where the design is going to show. When you are pleased with the look of it, take each piece or several at a time to the spray box.

I do not recommend pinning the designs. You cannot embroider with pins poking you, and it tends to distort the felt in the process. If you do not care for basting spray, you can use a thin layer of stick glue or you can baste them on with thread.

When using basting spray in the house, always spray into a spray box—you do not want to stick to the carpet or the floor from the overspray. And you don't want the cat to give you "the look" as if you had done it on purpose to ruin her life.

FABULOUS WOOL FELT

I made my spray box out of an ordinary cardboard box. I taped the flaps up to create a deeper box, then laid it on its side. You can also step outside and spray on a table covered with plastic or newspaper.

Do not use a hoop as it will stretch, tear and weaken the felt. Felt is stronger and firmer than fabric and will maintain its own shape. This will make you hoopless but not hopeless, so continue on.

Once you have placed your elements (by method of your choice) on your project, attach them with a buttonhole stitch or running stitch or another embroidery stitch that suits you.

After all the basic elements are attached, you can add vines, star embroidery, additional French knots, etc., to your project. Use the basting spray to layer all the background pieces together. This stabilizes your project and prevents them slipping during the rest of the embroidery work.

I steam press my project before doing the final edge to make sure everything is lined up and looks good. To finish, I used a buttonhole stitch around my entire project through all layers.

When I am finished, I apologize to the cat, take a quick bow and start on another wool-felted project. Enjoy!

List of Supplies

- *Felt
- Sharp scissors
- Freezer paper
- Basting spray (optional)
- Embroidery thread, a nice variety
- Embroidery needles
- Iron
- Ribbon
- Wool balls, hand made or store bought
- Embellishments of your choice, buttons, beads, charms, etc.
- Spray Box (a fancy name for a cardboard box for spraying pieces of felt and not getting the over spray on the floor)
- Chalk pencil
- New shoestring or cord

*You will get a world of opinions on felt, so let me share what I know about it.

100% Wool Felt - made from un-spun wool fibers called roving. It is available at some local craft stores and online. It is the highest priced, but if you are only buying 1/8 yard of all the colors you need, it becomes affordable.

Blended Wool Felt - a blend of wool and acrylic fibers 80/20 or 70/30 is available at your craft store and 50/50 blends are available online. This is the most affordable and the most widely used for wool felt projects.

Bamboo Felt - soft and lovely to work with and comes in a limited number of colors. It is priced about the same as the blended wool felt and performs just about the same. I was very impressed.

100% Acrylic Felt - Many people don't care for this product, but it works well if

6

FABULOUS WOOL FELT

it is thick and bought off the bolt. Give it a hot wash and hot dry, and it works well for lots of projects.

I have found some 100% acrylic felt with novelty prints on them and according to the Foss Manufacturing Company, their *ecofil* felt is made from recycled plastic bottles. Armed with that information and being a person who enjoys recycling, I decided to include a bookmark project made using that type of felt in this book.

Felted Wool - This is wool that has been spun into yarn and woven into shirts, skirts, etc. Items can be purchased in second hand shops and cut apart, over-dyed, then washed in hot water and dried in a hot dryer. Squares of various sizes can

be purchased online and some people felt their own wool at home.

Felted wool works well for accents. Be sure to check the edges for fraying so you can decide how you want to use it in your project. It is fun to add a plaid now and again.

All of these products work well with the projects in this book. Buy what you can afford and what suits your needs. I bought most of my wool felt at my local fabric store, and I ordered a few stacks of superb colors online for a low cost. And (I am whispering) I accidentally washed and shrunk one of my husband's wool shirts. Oops!

Embroidery Stitches

Chain Stitch

French Knot

Lazy Daisy Stitch

Stem Stitch

Straight Stitch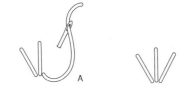

Star Stitch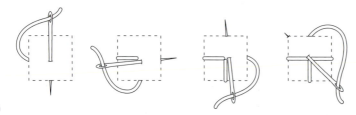

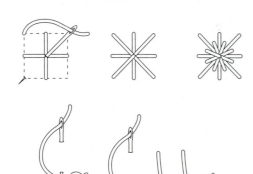

Buttonhole Stitch

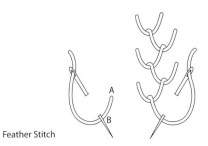

Feather Stitch

Use your favorite embroidery thread. Keep in mind that some over-dyed floss bleeds because it is not colorfast.

My favorite floss is 100% cotton, six-strand thread. I have also used number 8 or number 12 pearl cotton with great success.

I use two strands of floss and cut my thread to 18" lengths. That length is easy to handle and doesn't twist or knot as easily as longer lengths.

I use three strands of thread when making French knots for a fuller, rounder knot.

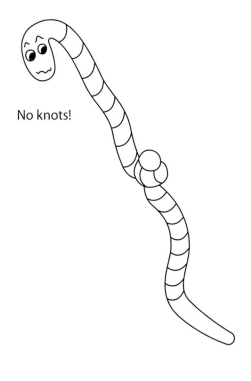

No knots!

Apple and Acorn Needle Keeps

These needle cases make great gifts for sewing friends. The inside tongue that holds the needles uses one layer of felt, all other pieces use two layers. You'll be using a running stitch, French knots and the buttonhole stitch.

APPLE

Finished Size: 4" x 5"

SUPPLY LIST

Wool Felt

- 1 – 8 1/2" square red
- 1 – 4" square brown
- Scrap of yellow
- Scrap of green

OTHER SUPPLIES

- Embroidery floss to match project elements
- Snap

DIRECTIONS

Refer to the templates on page 53 and cut the following shapes:

- 4 apples from red
- 2 stems and one tongue from brown
- 1 highlight from yellow
- 2 leaves from green

Refer to the general instructions on pages 4-5 and spray-baste the top layers of the apple together, the back layers, the leaves and the stem.

Stitch around the layered elements using a buttonhole stitch.

Place the back of the apple, the stem, leaf and top of the apple together and stitch along the top edge. Add the yellow highlight using a buttonhole stitch. Sew a snap to the inside top and bottom layers of the apple to complete the project.

FABULOUS WOOL FELT

ACORN

Finished Size: 3 1/2" x 6"

SUPPLY LIST

Wool Felt

- 1 – 4" x 5" square dark brown felt
- 1 – 3 1/3" x 6" rectangle light brown felt
- 1 – 3 1/2" x 6" rectangle brown plaid
- 1 – 3" square bright green
- Scrap of medium green

OTHER SUPPLIES

- Embroidery floss to match project elements
- Snap

DIRECTIONS

Refer to the templates on page 53 and cut the following shapes:

- 2 acorn caps from dark brown
- 2 acorn bases from light brown
- 2 acorn bases from brown plaid
- 1 tongue from bright green
- 2 leaves from medium green

Refer to the general instructions on pages 4-5 and spray-baste the top layers of the acorn base together using the plaid felt on the inside. Do the same for the back layer. Spray-baste the leaf layers together, as well.

Stitch around the layered elements using a buttonhole stitch.

Place the back of the acorn, the tongue, and the front of the acorn together and tuck them under the bottom edge of the acorn cap. Tuck the leaf between the layers of the top of the acorn cap and stitch everything together. Use a buttonhole stitch around the top and a running stitch around the bottom. Add four French knots to the upper left side of the acorn cap.

Stitch a snap to the inside of the acorn base layers to complete the project.

FABULOUS
WOOL
FELT

Eyeglass Cases

It is always nice to be able to find your glasses. Make one for each person who wears a pair of glasses in your family. These make great gifts for a friend or neighbor. Be sure you fold down one corner for easy access.

Finished Size: 3 1/2" x 7 1/4"

SUPPLY LIST

Wool Felt

- 2 – 8" squares
  (Choose two complimentary colors, one for the outside of the case, one for the inside.)

For case with flowers:

- 1 – 5" square light pink or color of your choice
- 1 – 3" square of green
- Scrap of medium pink
- Yellow embroidery floss

For fish:

- 1 – 3" x 4 1/2" dark brown, gray or light green
- Orange and green embroidery floss

For tie:

- 1 – 1 1/2" x 4" plaid or color of your choice
- Scrap for knot

DIRECTIONS

Refer to the templates on page 54 and cut the number of pieces needed for the eyeglass case you are making.

Spray-baste the front and back layers together. Make a mark 1 1/2" down from the top on the front side of the case. Fold in half and stitch the two pieces together using a buttonhole stitch. Begin sewing across the bottom, then go up the side until you arrive at your mark.

When you reach your mark, turn the corner down and stitch in place. Continue on around the top of the opening until you arrive back at your mark.

Appliqué the elements you have chosen in place using the buttonhole stitch. Add French knots where noted to complete your eyeglass case.

FABULOUS
WOOL
FELT

15

Trinket Box

This pretty little box is as handy as a pocket on a shirt. Toss in sewing supplies or little treasures you want to keep in a safe place.

Finished Size: 5 1/2" x 4 1/2" x 4"

SUPPLY LIST

Wool Felt

- 2 – 10" squares

Flowers

- 1 – 7 1/2" square red or your favorite color
- 1 – 3 1/2" square blue – large flower center
- 1 – 3" square yellow – small flower center

Leaves

- 1 – 6" square green – leaves

DIRECTIONS

Refer to the templates on page 55 and cut,

- 5 flowers
- 10 leaves
- 5 large circles
- 5 small circles

Place the two 10" squares together and mark a 5" square in the center of the inside square and sew a running stitch around the marked square using contrasting thread.

Center a flower motif and two leaves in the center of the inside square and appliqué in place using a running stitch.

Center and appliqué a flower motif and two leaves on each of the four outside edges of the box. Finish the outside edges with a buttonhole stitch.

To create the box, fold up the sides 2 1/2" from the center and pinch the corners together. Push the corners in toward the center and tack in place.

FABULOUS
WOOL
FELT

Distelfink Wall Hanging

(Thistle Finch)

Distelfink is a lovely, traditional Pennsylvania Dutch design that promises happiness and good fortune. The word literally translates to Thistle Finch.

Finished Size: 23" square

SUPPLY LIST

Background

2 – 26" x 24" rectangles

Hearts

- 1 – 8" x 6" rectangle red – large heart
- 1 – 3 1/2" x 5" rectangle yellow – contrasting heart

Leaves and Curley Qs

- 1 – 14" x 21" rectangle green

Flowers

- 1 – 4 1/2" x 6 1/2" rectangle dark purple (or your choice of color)
- 1 – 3 1/2" x 6" rectangle blue – flower tops

Distlefink (Bird)

- 1 – 9 1/2" x 10" rectangle yellow – body, beak, decorative circles
- 1 – 7 1/2" x 4 1/2" rectangle red – wing and head
- 1 – 3" x 5 ½" rectangle blue – for tail
- 1 – 3" x 6" rectangle white - strips on bird wing and tail

OTHER SUPPLIES

- Embroidery floss
  Yellow
  Light green
  Red
- Small dowel rod - 26" long

DIRECTIONS

From the background fabric, cut
2 – 26" x 24" rectangles

Refer to the templates on pages 56-58 and cut the pieces needed. Place the pieces on the top layer of the background fabric in a whimsical fashion while leaving 2" at the top unadorned. (You'll want that space open to fold over for the rod pocket.) Begin with the corner elements, then add the center pieces.

FABULOUS

WOOL

FELT

Placement of the vines is up to you – just have fun with those. French knots and the decorative circles were used randomly for decoration.

Spray-baste all elements to the top layer of the wall hanging. Attach the pieces using a buttonhole stitch or chain stitch.

Once all the pieces have been stitched in place and the embroidery work completed, turn it over and press the reverse side. Place the front and back pieces together. Buttonhole stitch around the sides and the bottom of the wall hanging. Use a running stitch through all the layers in a random pattern to add movement and to fasten them together.

Fold the top over to create a small rod pocket for the dowel rod. Use a running stitch to fasten the pocket in place. Add a ribbon to either side of the dowel rod as shown in the photo to complete your wall hanging.

Small Tablet Case

Your small tablet will be well protected in this cute little case.
Make one for yourself and another for a friend!

Finished Size: 7 1/4" x 9"

SUPPLY LIST

Wool Felt

- 2 – 7 1/4" x 12" rectangles – for back
- 2 – 7 1/4" x 9" rectangles – for front

Circles

- 1 – 3 1/4" square red – large circle
- 1 – 2 1/4" square cream – medium circle
- 1 – 2 3/4" square yellow – small circle and drop
- 1 – 1 1/2 square blue – drop
- 1 – 1 1/2 square pink – drop

OTHER SUPPLIES

- Black embroidery floss
- Snap

DIRECTIONS

Refer to the templates on pages 59-60 and cut the pieces needed.

Spray-baste the pieces to the top front layer of the case. Stitch the circle design and the drops in place using the buttonhole stitch. Using black embroidery floss to make a stem stitch, connect the drops to the circle design.

Place the two top layers together and stitch across the top using the buttonhole stitch.

Place the two back layers together with the two front layers. Stitch all around the case using a buttonhole stitch. Sew the snap on to the flap and the front of the case.

Star Candle Mat

If you need a star to wish on, we have one right here for you.
This fun little mat makes a perfect home for your favorite candle.

Finished Size: 11"

SUPPLY LIST

Wool Felt

Background
- 2 – 11" squares blue

Top
- 1 – 9 1/2" square black

Stars
- 8 – 3" squares – assorted colors

OTHER SUPPLIES

- Embroidery floss
  8 colors – match each star
  Black
  Blue
- Chalk Pencil

DIRECTIONS

Refer to the templates on pages 61-62
and cut the required pieces.

Place pattern piece D in the center of the
top of the candle mat pattern piece B. Using
the chalk pencil, draw around the circle. Use
a running stitch to embroider the marked
circle. You will have this free space for a
candle.

Spray-baste all the stars in place and stitch
them down using a buttonhole stitch.
Thread a large-eye needle with 8 strands of
embroidery thread, one for each color of the
stars, and using the daisy chain stitch, weave
the stitches in and out of the stars.

Sew the completed top B piece to a background A piece, using the buttonhole stitch.
Now add the last background A piece and
stitch the layers together using the buttonhole stitch to complete the mat.

FABULOUS
WOOL
FELT

Snap Tablet

This handy little notepad fits right into a purse. And that's a good thing for me because I make notes about everything. I also use it as a sketch pad when the inspiration for another project travels into my head.

Finished Size: 3 3/4" x 5"

SUPPLY LIST

Wool Felt

- Outer and inner cover
  1 – 12 3/4" x 3 3/4" rectangle tan
  1 – 12 3/4" x 3 3/4" rectangle red
  1 – 5" x 3 3/4" rectangle black

Appliquéd Flower

- 1 – 1 1/2" x 2 1/2" rectangle red
- 1 – 2 1/2" square light green
- Scrap of dark green

OTHER SUPPLIES

- Embroidery floss
  Red
  Tan
  Green
- 1 med snap

DIRECTIONS

Refer to the templates on page 63 and cut the required number of pieces.

Spray-baste or pin the flower and leaves in place onto the outside layer. Appliqué them in place using the buttonhole stitch. Pin the single layer support piece 5" up from the bottom of the inside layer. Pin the three layers together and sew around the outer edge using the buttonhole stitch.

Add a snap to complete the tablet cover.

*Before you start this project, check your local office supply store for inexpensive scratch pads. You may have to adjust your pattern size to fit your notepad.

FABULOUS
WOOL
FELT

Hands On Wall Hanging

This project is so much fun for the whole family! It can be a wall hanging or a table runner. While the hanging we made was 34" long, the number of hands you add will determine the size you make. Be prepared to adjust your fabric requirements to accommodate any changes.

Finished Size: 13" x 34"

SUPPLY LIST

Wool Felt
- Background
  13" x 36" red
  13" x 34" tan
  10" x 31" green

Hands
- Skin tone or bright colors of your choice
  – the amount needed is determined by
  the size of the hands used.

Flowers
- 1 – 5" x 7" rectangle dark purple
- 1 – 3" x 4" rectangle light purple
- 1 – 3" x 4" rectangle yellow

Leaves
- 1 – 5" x 7" rectangle
- Scraps, buttons, ribbon, or other
  small items for embellishments

OTHER SUPPLIES
- Embroidery floss
  Yellow
  Medium green
  Tan
- Freezer paper
- Small dowel rod for wall hanging

DIRECTIONS

If you are planning on making this project for a table runner, you will need to round both ends of the project. (I used a dinner plate.) If you are using it for a wall hanging, you will need to cut the top straight across and make a rod pocket. To make the rod pocket, fold the longer end of the red (back layer) over to the front. Use a running stitch across the top. Slide a small dowel rod through the pocket.

Have family/friends trace their hands onto the dull side of freezer paper. Write

FABULOUS
WOOL
FELT

CONTINUED ON PAGE 28

the name of the person and a list of interests, hobbies or talents on the paper to
remind you which pattern belongs to which
person. Iron the slick side of the paper pattern to the wool for easy cutting.

Cut out the hands and decorate each with
embellishments that represent that person.
Use buttons, jewels, lace, old keys, beads,
feathers, etc. Use your imagination and
have fun with this.

When you are finished decorating the
hands, attach them to the green layer with
a buttonhole stitch.

Sew the green layer to the tan, again using
the buttonhole stitch. Add the last red layer, using the same stitch. If you are making
the wall hanging, remember to leave the
opening for the rod pocket on each side.

Refer to the templates on page 64 and cut
out the leaves and flowers. Stitch the vine,
using a lazy daisy stitch, then add the flowers and leaves in a whimsical fashion. Refer
to the photo for placement purposes if necessary, keeping in mind that your project
may be a different size than the one shown.

Bookmarks

Bookmarks are always welcome for those of us who love to read. These fabulous, patterned ones stand out and are not easily lost.

Finished Size: 2" x 7"

SUPPLY LIST

Wool Felt*

- 1 – 4" x 7" rectangle color of your choice for each bookmark
- Embroidery floss to match or contrast with background
- Wool felt balls or buttons

DIRECTIONS

Cut the rectangle in half lengthwise. Place the two pieces, one atop the other, and stitch them together using the buttonhole stitch.

Braid three strands of embroidery thread together and sew cute buttons or a wool-felted ball to one end. Attach the other end to the bookmark.

*I used a product called ECO-FI, a polyester felt by the Foss Manufacturing Company who states it is made from recycled post-consumer plastic bottles, so it is my ultimate choice for polyester felt. It's an excellent product for those who like to recycle.

Carrot Scissor Holder and Fobs

We want to take good care of our scissors and protect them from damage.
This playful little carrot is up to the task and is bright enough
to be noticed even in a crowd of stitchers.

LARGE CARROT

Finished Size: 4" x 10"

SUPPLY LIST

Wool Felt

- 2 – 10" x 4 1/4" rectangles orange
- 2 – 3 1/2" x 8" rectangles orange
- 2 – 4" x 4 1/2" rectangles dark green
- Scraps of light green

OTHER SUPPLIES

- Embroidery floss
  Orange
  Green
- Snap

DIRECTIONS

Refer to the templates on pages 65-66. Cut two full-size carrot pieces from the orange wool for the back of the case and two carrot bottoms for the front. From the green felt, cut two carrot tops.

Sew the bottom halves of the carrot to the green tops using the buttonhole stitch. Spray-baste the two fronts together and use a running stitch for the lines on the bottom of the carrot. Add highlights to the green carrot top.

Spray-baste the two carrot backs together.

Stitch the front of the carrot to the back using a buttonhole stitch. Begin stitching at the base of the leaves, continue on around until you reach the other side of the leaves. Buttonhole stitch around the front layer separately, then finish the back top of the carrot with the buttonhole stitch. This will leave the top of the carrot open so the scissors can slip inside. Sew a snap at the top to keep your scissors inside.

FABULOUS
WOOL
FELT

Here are a couple of little fobs to put on your scissors. Make them from scraps and add a little ribbon and you're done!

CARROT FOB

Finished Size: 1 1/2" x 4"

SUPPLY LIST

Wool Felt

- 1 – 1 1/2" x 3" rectangle orange
- 1 – 2" square green

OTHER SUPPLIES

- 6" length ribbon
- Embroidery floss
  Green
  Orange

DIRECTIONS

Refer to the templates on page 65 and cut one carrot bottom and one carrot top. Sew the top to the bottom using a buttonhole stitch. Fold the ribbon in half and stitch it to the top of the fob.

ROUND SCISSOR FOB

Finished Size: 2"

SUPPLY LIST

Wool Felt

- Orange and green scraps
- 6" length of ribbon
- Carrot button

DIRECTIONS

Refer to the templates on page 65 and cut the necessary pieces. Place the elements as shown and stitch them together using the buttonhole stitch. Add a length of ribbon and sew in place. Complete the fob by sewing a carrot button to the center.

Mug Rug

If you're looking for a quick gift to make for a friend or neighbor, this mug rug is perfect.

Finished Size: 10 1/4" x 5 3/4"

SUPPLY LIST

Wool Felt

Background
- 2 – 10 1/4" x 5 3/4" rectangles

Leaves
- 2 – 3" squares green

Acorns
- 2 – 2" squares light brown
- 2 – 2" squares dark brown

OTHER SUPPLIES

- Embroidery floss
  Green
  Brown

DIRECTIONS

Refer to the templates on page 67 and cut out the necessary appliqué pieces. Spray-baste or pin the acorns to the top layer of background wool. Sew in place using the buttonhole stitch.

Place the appliquéd top on the bottom rectangle and use a buttonhole stitch around the outer edge after rounding all the corners. Use a running stitch in a random pattern to add movement and to fasten the layers together.

Hoppy the Rooster Table Mat

Hens, chicks and roosters have long been favored motifs for the kitchen. Our rooster, Hoppy, is a bright, cheerful boy who will be ready to greet you as you sit at the table with your first cup of coffee. He'll be proud to let you show off a variety of embroidery stitches.

Finished Size: 26" x 16 1/2"

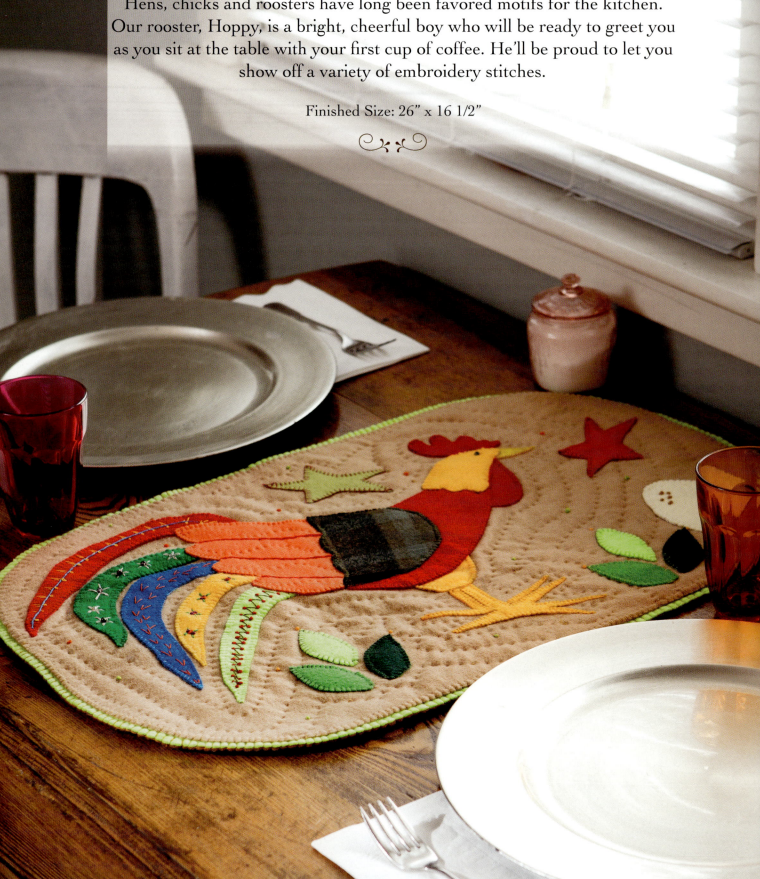

In the introduction I mentioned that I had accidently washed and shrunk my husband's wool shirt. As if that wasn't bad enough, I accidentally over dyed it green. These things happen and in the spirit of recycle and repurpose, I used it in my favorite project, hence guilt-free felting.

SUPPLY LIST

Wool Felt

Background
- 2 – 26" x 16 1/2" rectangles pale green
- 1 – 25 3/4" x 16 1/4" rectangle tan

Rooster
- 1 – 9 ½" square red – body, wattle, comb, tail feather No. 1
- 1 – 7" x 2 1/2" rectangle light green – tail feather No. 5
- 1 – 7" x 2 1/2" rectangle blue – tail feather No. 3
- 1 – 8" x 4 1/2 rectangle medium green – tail feather No. 2
- 1 – 10" x 12" rectangle deep yellow – feet, upper leg, tail feather No. 4, head
- 1 – 5 1/2" square orange – lower wing feathers
- 1 – 3 1/2" x 5" rectangle plaid – lower wing
- Scrap of yellow – beak

Stars
- 1 – 4" x 5" rectangle red
- 1 – 4" x 5" rectangle green

Leaves
- 1 – 3" square light green
- 1 – 3" square medium green
- 1 – 3" square dark green

Egg
- 1 – 3 1/4" x 4 1/4" rectangle beige

OTHER SUPPLIES
- **Embroidery floss**
  Tan
  Green
  Red
  Yellow
  Blue
  Orange

DIRECTIONS

Cut two 26" x 16 1/2" rectangles from the green background fabric and round the edges using a dinner plate for a template. Sew the two layers together using a buttonhole stitch.

Cut one 25 3/4" x 16 1/4" rectangle tan for the top layer. All appliqué elements should be placed on this layer.

Refer to the templates on pages 68-72 and cut the needed pieces. Spray-baste the pieces to the tan background in a whimsical fashion. Sew them in place using a buttonhole stitch.

Embellish the tail feathers with stitches of your choice. Refer to pages 4-5 for stitch examples.

Attach the appliquéd layer to the green layers using the buttonhole stitch and a contrasting color of embroidery floss.

Use a running stitch in a random pattern to add movement and to fasten the three layers together.

FABULOUS
WOOL
FELT

Tea Cozy

When I was growing up, my family owned a "tear drop" trailer, which I loved. It was my little house in the woods. Every time I see this tea cozy, it brings a smile to my face.

Finished Size: 16" x 10"

SUPPLY LIST

Wool Felt

Background

- 4 – 16" x 10" rectangles beige
- 4 – 4" squares black – tires
- 4 – 2" squares grey – hubcaps
- 2 – 3" x 1 1/4" rectangles blue – awning bases
- 4 – 1" squares white – awnings
- 1 – 2" square light blue – window
- 1 – 2 3/4" x 3/4" rectangle – window box
- 2 – 2 1/2" x 3" rectangles dark blue – bird
- 2 – 16" x 3/4" strips teal for lower part of the tea cozy
- 1 – 6" x 2 1/4" rectangle brown – door
- 1 – 2 1/2"5 1/2" rectangles black – back design
- Scraps for beak, flowers and leaves

OTHER SUPPLIES

- Shank button
- Embroidery floss

  Tan

  Blue

  Grey

  Pink

  Green

DIRECTIONS

Refer to the templates on pages 73-75 and cut all pattern pieces. Spray-baste all the pieces in place except the wheels and the bird to the outer layer of the cozy, and stitch in place with a buttonhole stitch. The teal strips should be placed on the front and the back where noted on the template. Attach the leaves and flowers to the window box with French knots. Notice that the awning over the window and door is made by appliquéing the white pieces over the blue base.

After you have completed the appliqué work, sew the tea cozy together using a buttonhole stitch. When you have finished sewing the sides together, stitch around the bottom edge. Add the shanked button for the doorknob. Sew several lines of running stitches through the front layers and the back layers to fasten them together.

Stitch two black circles together to make each tire. Attach a tire to the front of the cozy by sewing the hubcap on through all front layers; repeat on the back of the tea cozy.

Stitch the layers of the bird's beak together and insert it into the bird's head. Attach the beak using a running stitch. Stitch around the bird with buttonhole stitch but leave the bottom open. Perch the bird on top of the cozy and secure with a buttonhole stitch.

The design included for the back is a swirl, but you can use your initials or a flower if it pleases you.

FABULOUS
WOOL
FELT

Thistle Penny Rug

I adore penny rugs. As most people know, penny rugs are not actually rugs, unless you live in a wee little house and step lively. Instead they are used as decorative mats on tables, dressers or mantles.

Finished Size: 20 1/2" x 16"

SUPPLY LIST

Wool Felt

- Background
  3 – 15" x 10 1/2" squares

Thistles

- 1 – 20" x 15" rectangle dark green
- 1 – 6" x 6 1/2" dark purple

Pennies (Circles)

- 8 – 10" squares – choose different colors that will blend

OTHER SUPPLIES

- Embroidery floss
  to match wool felt
- 20 small buttons

DIRECTIONS

Refer to the templates on page 76 and cut out the pieces of the thistle. Appliqué the thistle pieces to the top layer of the background felt. Round the corners of the mat. A cup works great as a template. Stitch the three layers together using a buttonhole stitch. Use a running stitch through all three layers in a random pattern to add movement and to fasten the three layers together.

Cut two large circles, one medium and one small for each "penny." Attach a small circle to a medium and then attach to a large circle. Back each penny with a large circle. Place the pennies around the edge, and whipstitch the first one to the mat. Sew the next one in place by whip stitching the edge of the penny to the first, then to the mat. Continue on in this manner until all the pennies have been stitched in place. Add small buttons to the center of each penny for color.

FABULOUS
WOOL
FELT

Sewing Mat

I love to have a sewing mat beside me when I hand sew…
everything is at my fingertips.

Finished Size: 10"

SUPPLY LIST

Wool Felt

- Background
  2 – 11" squares green

Top

- 1 – 9 1/2" square teal

Scissor Holder

- 1 – 4 1/2" x 6" rectangle green

Pin Cushion

- 2 – 6" circles tan
- 7 – small red wool balls
- 1 – 3" red wool ball
- 1 – 3" circle cardboard
- 1 – 3" length ribbon

Needle Keep

- 1 – 4" x 2 1/4" rectangle tan
- 1 – 2" square your choice of color
  for thread

Thimble Holder

- 1 – 9" x 7 1/2" square magenta
- 1 – 3 1/2" x 6" rectangle plastic canvas

OTHER SUPPLIES

- 6" length of narrow ribbon
- 3 snaps
- Embroidery floss
  Green
  Teal
  Red
  Tan
  Purple
  Yellow

FABULOUS
WOOL
FELT

DIRECTIONS

The base of this mat is based on the candle mat pattern. Refer to the pattern on page 61 and cut out the pieces needed for the three layers of the base of the mat. Sew the layers together using a buttonhole stitch.

Refer to page 77 and cut out the elements needed for the mat.

Begin sewing the scissor holder to the mat about 2" down from the top of the layers with a buttonhole stitch. Continue on around until you are even with the first side. Sew around the remaining edge, leaving the top open. Put your scissors inside and place a snap so it will function in a loop of the scissors handle. The snap will prevent the scissors from falling out.

To make the pincushion, place the two 6" tan circles together and buttonhole stitch around the top edges to bind them together. Pinch up the side of the 6" circle and put a ball in and run a stitch into the felt and through the ball and out the side of the felt. Do this 6 more times.

Place a 3" cardboard circle in the bottom before you attach the center of the pincushion. This will keep the pins from coming through the entire mat. Place the large red wool ball over the cardboard and tack it to the outer part.

Buttonhole stitch the two layers of the spool needle keep together. Sew the piece you have chosen for the thread onto the top of the spool. Attach a ribbon to the spool and other end into the pincushion. Tack the spool down to the mat.

Sew one end of the length of narrow ribbon to the mat, and add a snap to the other end after adjusting the length so it fits through your spool of thread.

The three-sided thimble holder is a squeezebox. Decorate two of the sides of the wool felt wedges. Use the plastic canvas as the center layer of each wedge. Buttonhole stitch around each wedge to bind the layers together. Sew the two decorated wedges to either side of the third one, thus creating the three-sided squeeze shape. Open the squeezebox and stitch the bottom to the mat. Sew a snap on the two inside top edges to close it and secure your thimble.

Stitch decorative stars on the base of the mat in a random fashion to keep the three layers together.

FABULOUS
WOOL
FELT

The Sewing Heart

This goes to the very heart of taking your sewing tools
with you while away from home.

Finished Size: 8" x 9"

SUPPLY LIST

Wool Felt

Heart

- 5 – 8 1/2" squares orange
- 1 – 3 1/2" x 2 1/2" rectangle orange
- 5 – 8 1/2" squares tan
- 2 – 2" squares dark green
- 1 – 8 1/2" x 7" rectangle lime green
- 1 – 6" x 7" rectangle white
- 1 – 6" square teal
- 1 – 3" square dark blue

Pincushion

- 1 – 4" square blue

Thimble Pocket

- 1 – 3" x 3 1/2" rectangle blue piece
- 1 – 4 1/2" x 3 1/2" rectangle brown
- 1 – 3 1/2" x 1 1/2" for snap tab

Measuring Tape Pocket

- 1 – 4" x 2" rectangle pink

Scissor Holder

- 2 – 4 1/2" x 6" rectangles red

Pencil and Tweezers Pocket

- 1 – 4 3/4" x 2" rectangle red

Leaves

- Scraps of green

Spool Needle Keep

- 2 – 4" x 2 1/4" rectangle tan
- 1 – 2" square your choice of color
  for thread

OTHER SUPPLIES

- Accent ribbon for decoration
- Cardboard circle
- 3 Snaps – 1 large, 2 small
- Button

- Embroidery floss
  Orange
  Blue
  Green
  Red
  Pink

FABULOUS
WOOL
FELT

DIRECTIONS

Refer to the templates on pages 78-80 and cut out 10 hearts. Make two hearts three layers thick and two hearts two layers thick. Buttonhole stitch around each layered heart. You will have four hearts, two of them two layers thick and two of them three layers thick.

Fold each of the two layer hearts in half and buttonhole stitch from the heart dip to the bottom on the inside layer. This will cause a permanent crease in the heart and will fold in when the heart is closed. Set aside.

Refer to the templates on pages 78 and cut out the appliqué pieces for the feathers. Layer the feathers and use a buttonhole stitch to fasten each layer to the next. When all five feathers are complete, stitch them to the front heart. Refer to the photo if necessary. Decorate the back heart with simple embroidered stars, or use a running stitch in a random pattern to fasten the three layers together. Add the snap tab to the back of heart, making sure it will fold over and snap to the front heart where the other half of the snap will be sewn on.

Inside each panel of the heart are tool holders. Refer to the templates on pages 78-80 and cut the needed pieces. Refer to the photo on page 43 and sew the tool holders in place using a buttonhole stitch.

These are simple shapes and you can customize the holder to fit your needs. Be sure to put a piece of cardboard under your pincushion to keep your pins from poking through to the outside. Add a snap on the scissor holder and the thimble holder.

Lay the heart out on a table and mark with chalk exactly where the edges hit the next heart. Following your marks, buttonhole stitch the heart together from that mark to the bottom of the heart. After all the hearts are attached to each other and you've made sure it closes properly with the sides folding in, cut two 1 3/4" dark green end circles. Sew one of the circles to the center inside and one to the center outside.

FABULOUS
WOOL
FELT

Pattern Keeper

Have you ever wondered what to do with all those pattern pieces
you cut out for your projects? Here's the perfect solution
to that problem, the Pattern Keeper!

Finished Size: 11 1/2" x 12"

SUPPLY LIST

Wool Felt

Front and Back Covers
- 2 – 11 1/2" x 12" rectangles black
- 4 – 11 1/2" x 12" rectangles tan
- 5 – 1" x 12" strips blue
- 1 – 4" x 1 1/2" blue

Dragonflies
- 5 – 4" x 3 1/4" rectangles –
  your choice of colors

Plastic Canvas
- 2 – 11 1/2" x 1" rectangles

OTHER SUPPLIES

- 1 large snap
- 1 bootlace 45" long
- 10 plastic zip bags

DIRECTIONS

Sew the blue strips to the front layer of the
keeper. Refer to page 81 for the dragon-
fly pattern and cut five of various colors.
Stitch them in place, and add French knots
for the eyes, and use a running stitch for
the feelers.

Sew the three layers for the front together
with a buttonhole stitch. Do the same with
the back cover.

With a sharp hole punch, punch out five
holes in the front and back of the keeper.
Bind the holes with a buttonhole stitch.
Align the plastic canvas strips with the
cover and punch holes in the plastic canvas
to match the holes in the cover.

FABULOUS
WOOL
FELT

Stagger the 10 zip bags, beginning with two full sized. Add two bags one inch below and so on until all bags are staggered. Pin these bags at the bottom of the shortest bag. Cut off the excess. While still pinned, punch holes in the plastic bags at the same intervals as the plastic canvas and the front and back of the keeper. Keep the bags pinned together; you will remove the pins as you thread the keeper together.

Lay the back cover of the keeper down on a flat surface. Place the plastic canvas strip over the holes, making sure the holes line up. Layer the stack of plastic bags and the other strip of plastic canvas. Start the boot lace from behind the keeper. Pull the lace up through the back cover, canvas and the top

hole in the plastic bags, and the second strip of plastic canvas.

Remove the pins from the bags as you go. Place the front cover on top and thread the bootlace through to the front cover. Pull the lace up and make the back lace and front lace the same length. Using the top length of the bootlace, go through the second hole of the front of the keeper, catching all layers.

Thread from front to back and continue until you have laced to the bottom of the keeper. Bring the back cord over the top of the keeper and down through the first hole. Weave the lace in and out until both cords are at the bottom. Tie a secure bow to complete the project.

FABULOUS
WOOL
FELT

FABULOUS WOOL FELT

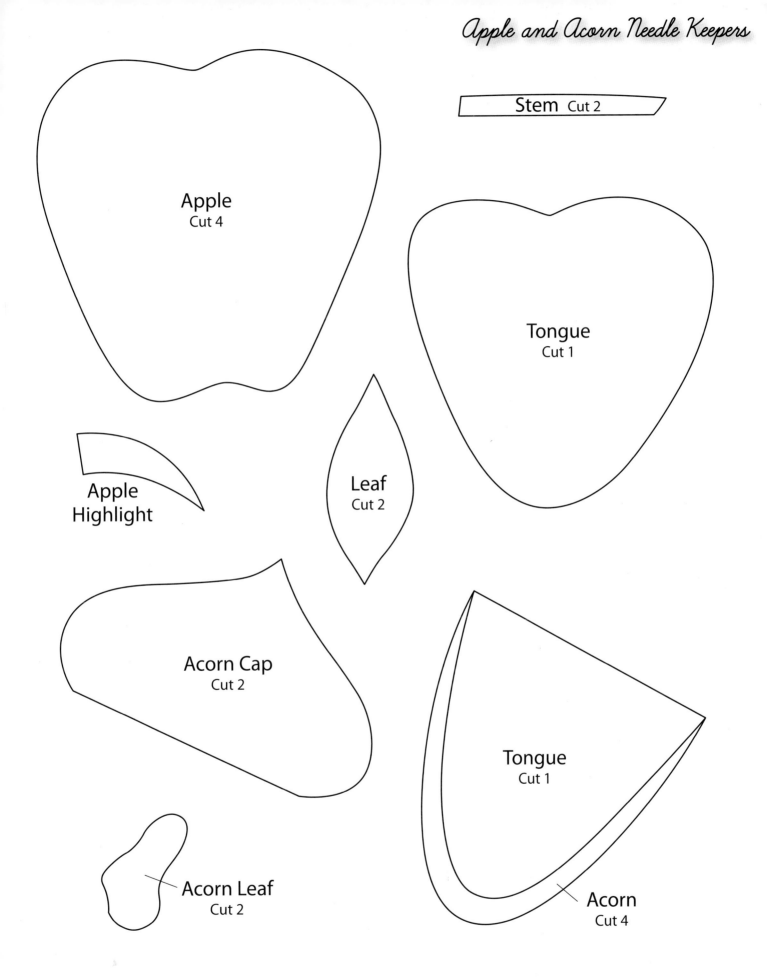

Apple
Cut 4

Stem Cut 2

Tongue
Cut 1

Apple
Highlight

Leaf
Cut 2

Acorn Cap
Cut 2

Tongue
Cut 1

Acorn Leaf
Cut 2

Acorn
Cut 4

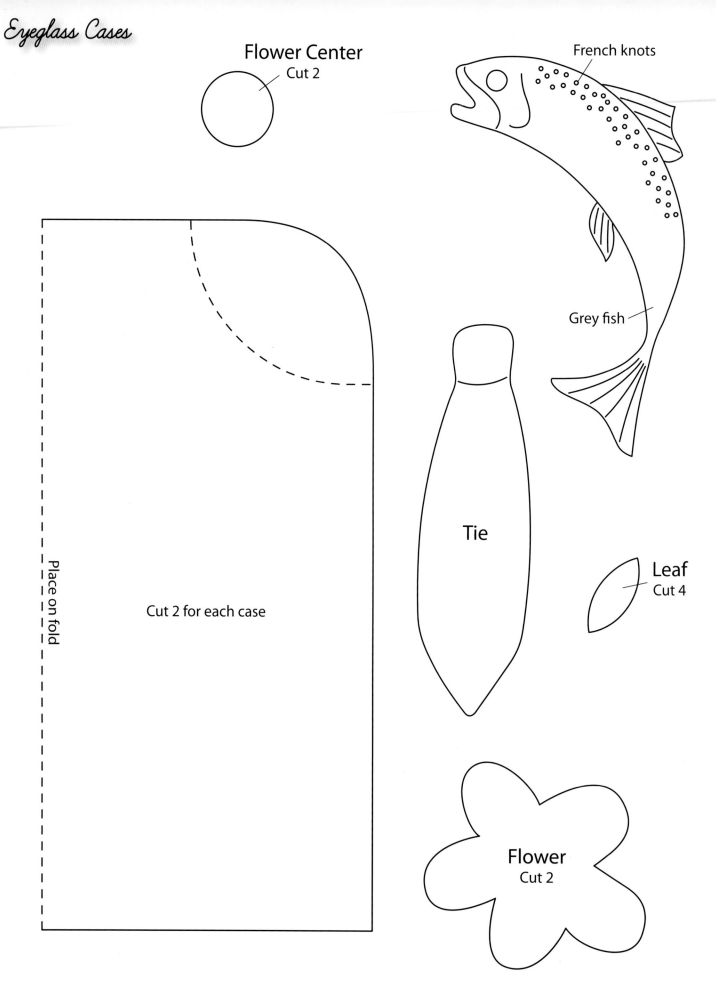

Flower Center
Cut 2

French knots

Grey fish

Place on fold

Cut 2 for each case

Tie

Leaf
Cut 4

Flower
Cut 2

FABULOUS WOOL FELT

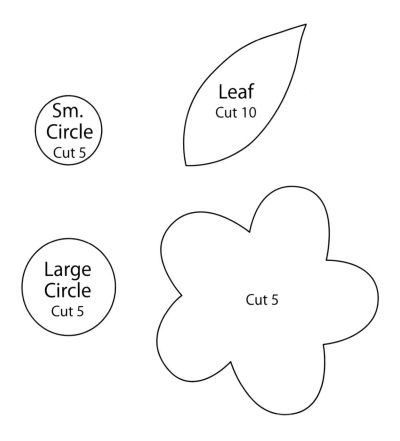

Sm.
Circle
Cut 5

Leaf
Cut 10

Large
Circle
Cut 5

Cut 5

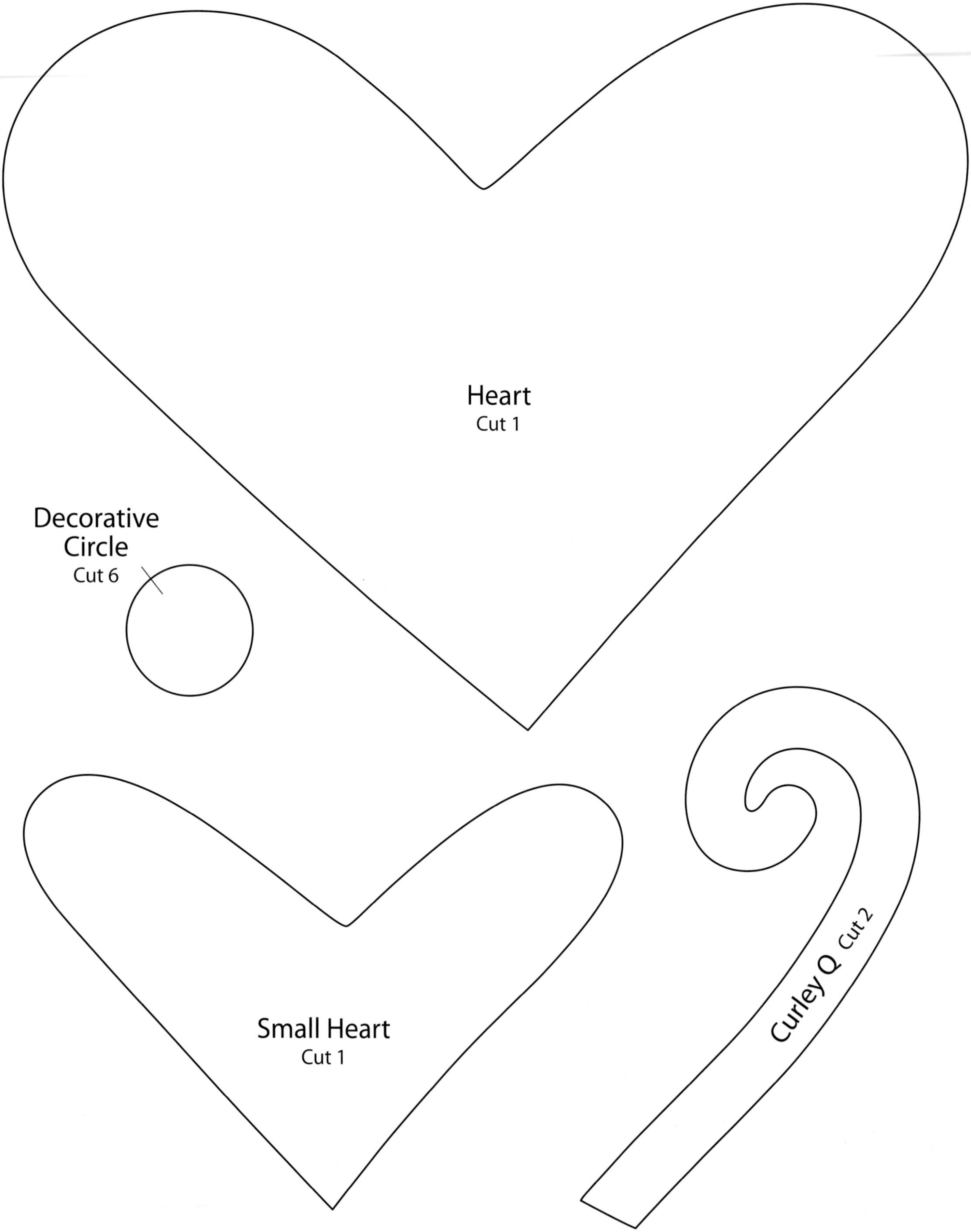

Heart
Cut 1

Decorative
Circle
Cut 6

Small Heart
Cut 1

Curley Q Cut 2

FABULOUS WOOL FELT

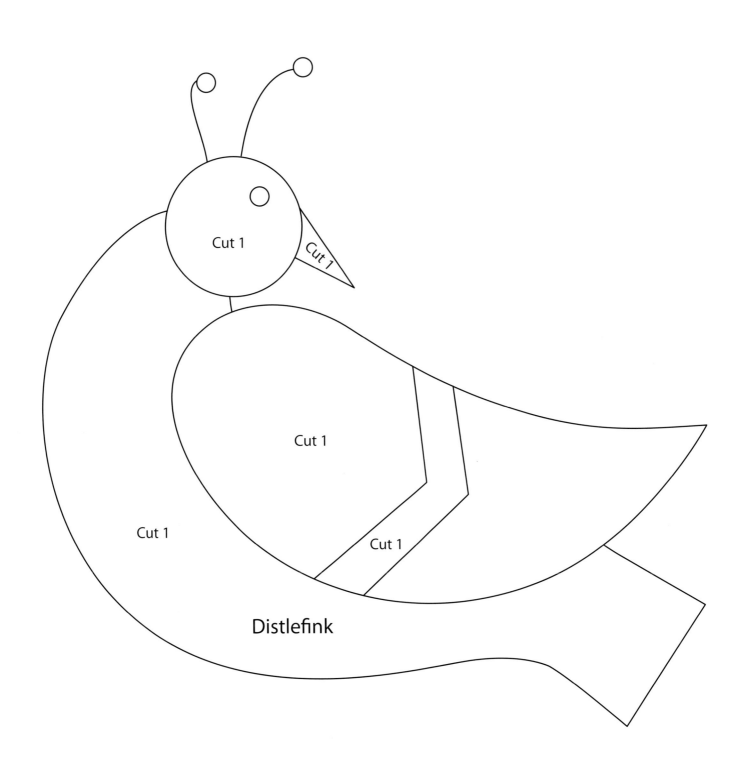

Cut 1

Cut 1

Cut 1

Cut 1

Cut 1

Distlefink

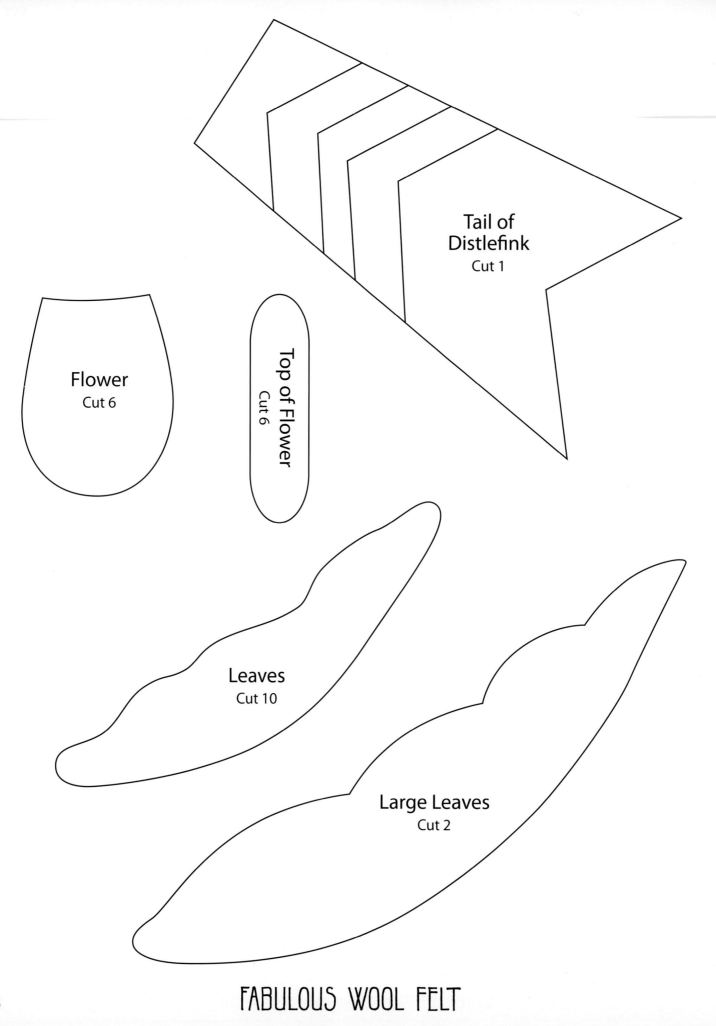

Tail of
Distlefink
Cut 1

Flower
Cut 6

Top of Flower
Cut 6

Leaves
Cut 10

Large Leaves
Cut 2

FABULOUS WOOL FELT

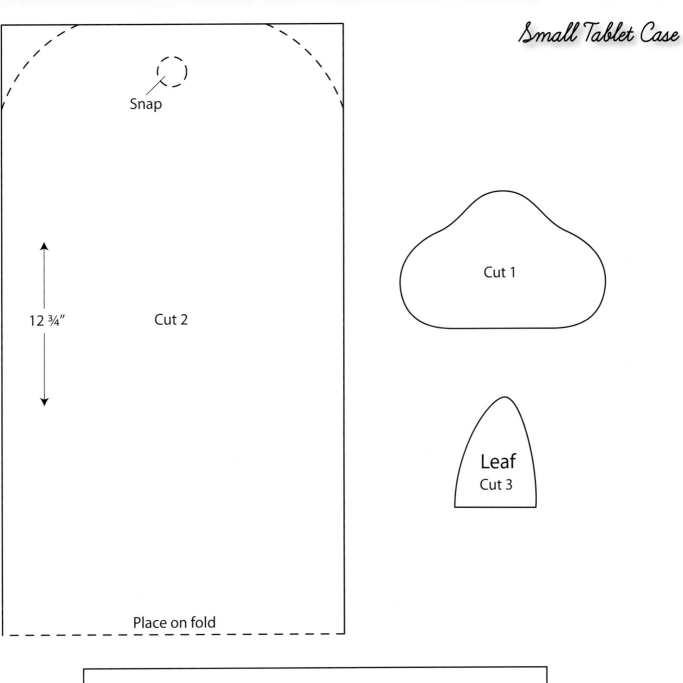

Snap

12 ¾"

Cut 2

Cut 1

Leaf
Cut 3

Place on fold

5" x 3¼"

Inner piece to hold tablet

Cut 2

Stitch 17 Fun Gifts and Projects

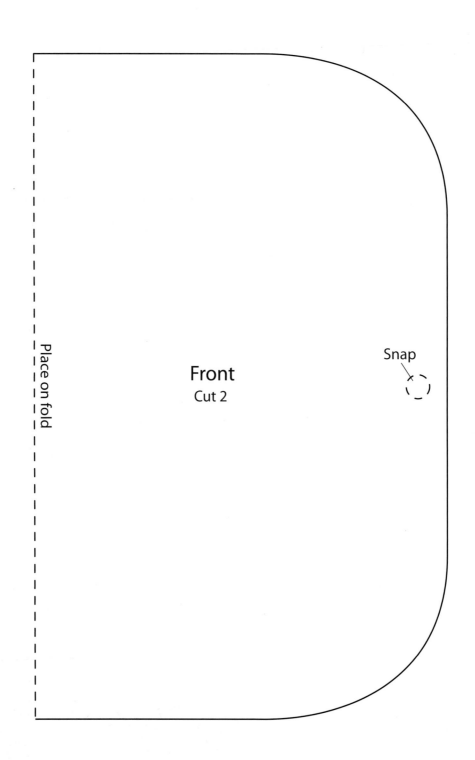

Place on fold

Snap

Front
Cut 2

FABULOUS WOOL FELT

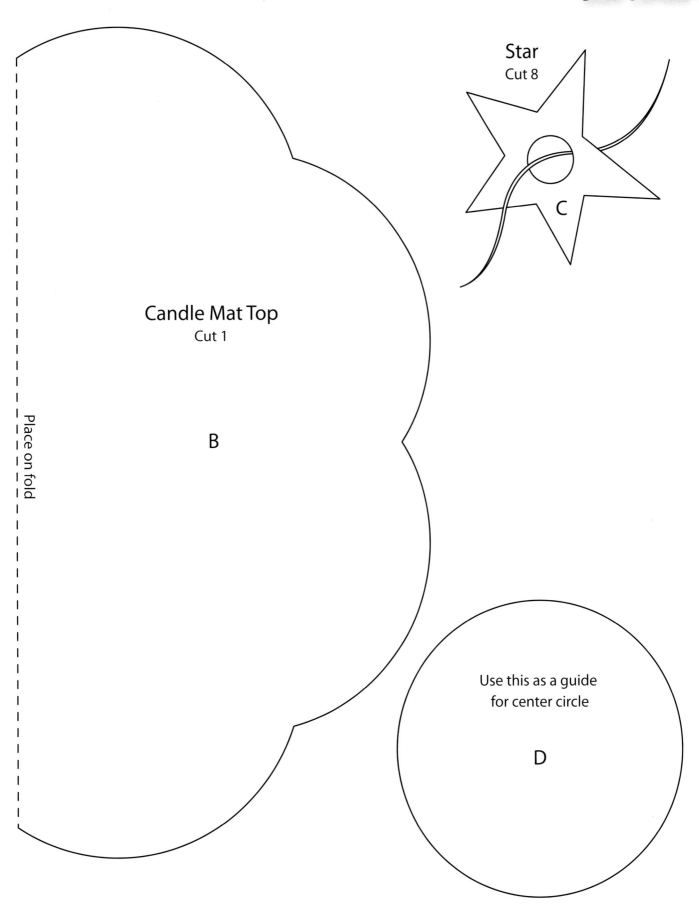

Star
Cut 8

C

Candle Mat Top
Cut 1

B

Place on fold

Use this as a guide
for center circle

D

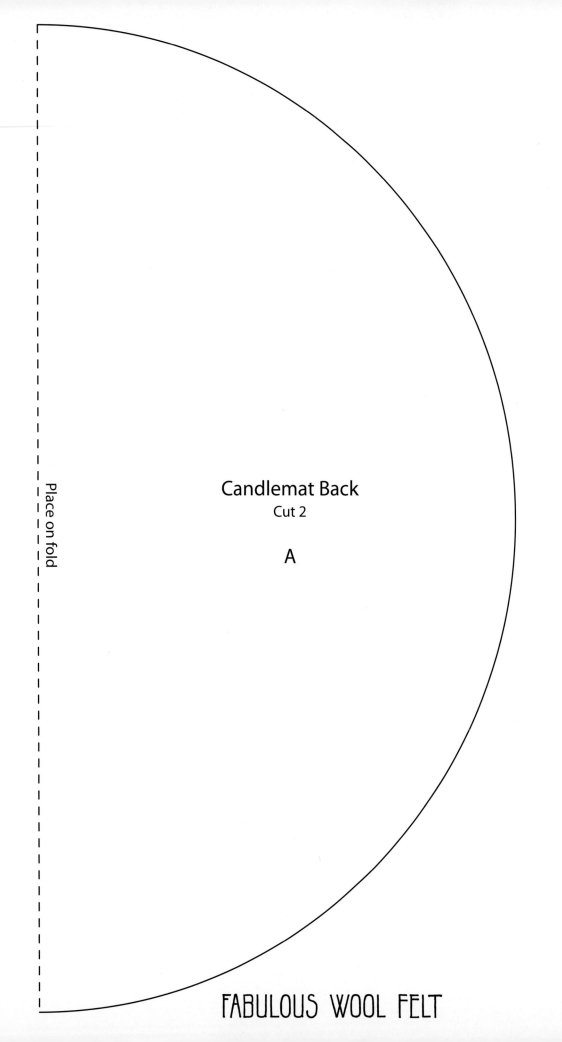

Place on fold

Candlemat Back
Cut 2

A

FABULOUS WOOL FELT

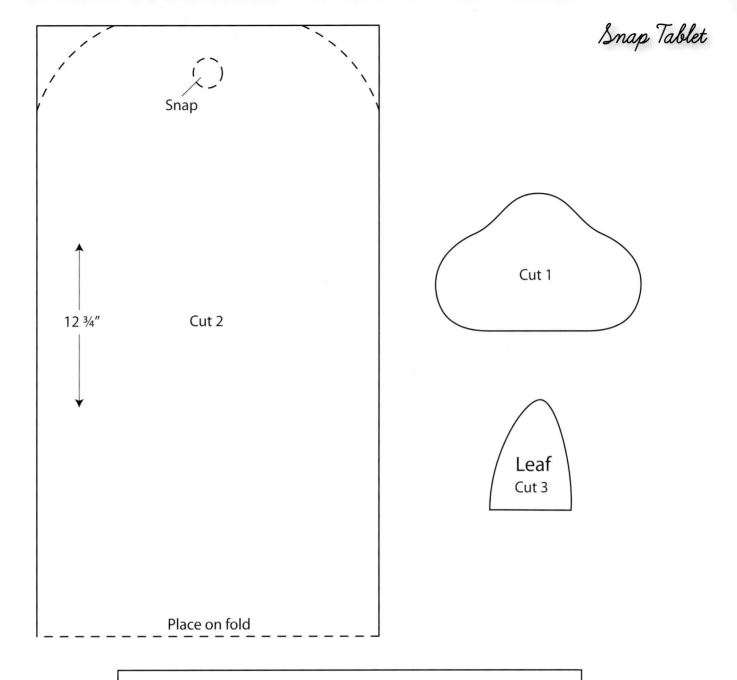

Snap

12 ¾"

Cut 2

Cut 1

Leaf
Cut 3

Place on fold

5" x 3¼"

Inner piece to hold tablet
Cut 2

Stitch 17 Fun Gifts and Projects

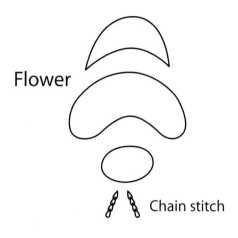

Flower

Chain stitch

Quantity of flower is
determined by length
of banner/mat

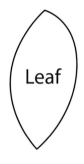

Leaf

FABULOUS WOOL FELT

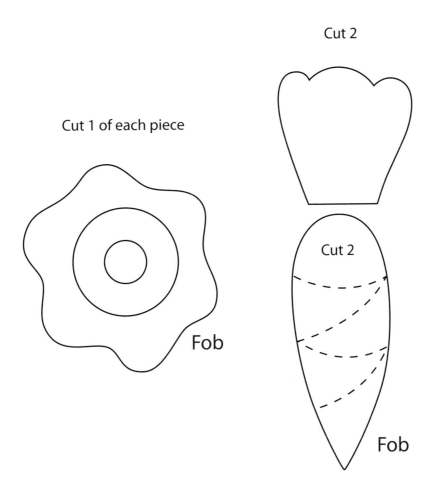

Cut 2

Cut 1 of each piece

Fob

Cut 2

Fob

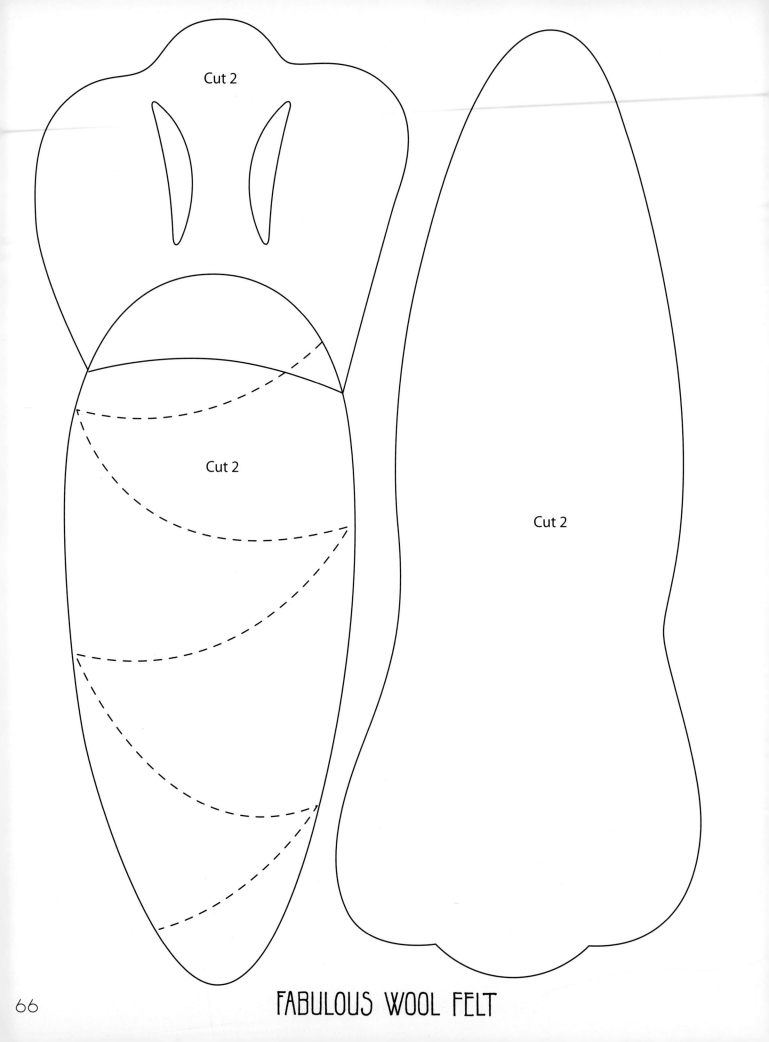

Cut 2

Cut 2

Cut 2

FABULOUS WOOL FELT

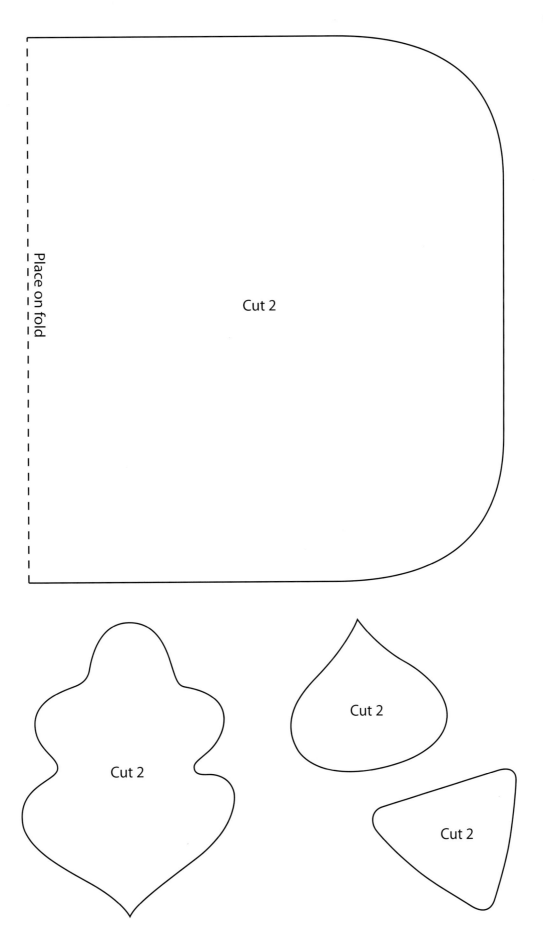

Place on fold

Cut 2

Cut 2

Cut 2

Cut 2

Stitch 17 Fun Gifts and Projects

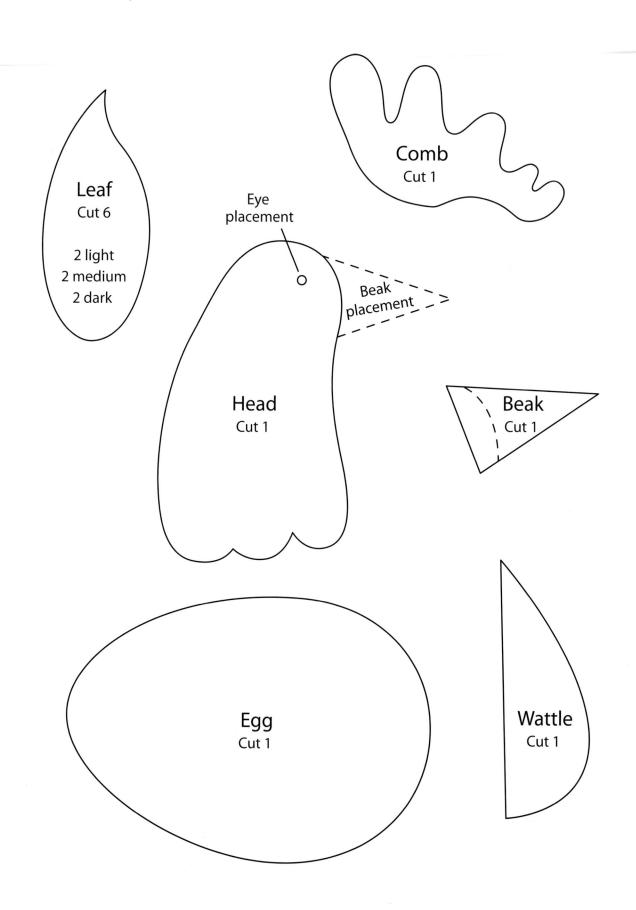

Leaf
Cut 6

2 light
2 medium
2 dark

Comb
Cut 1

Eye
placement

Beak
placement

Head
Cut 1

Beak
Cut 1

Egg
Cut 1

Wattle
Cut 1

FABULOUS WOOL FELT

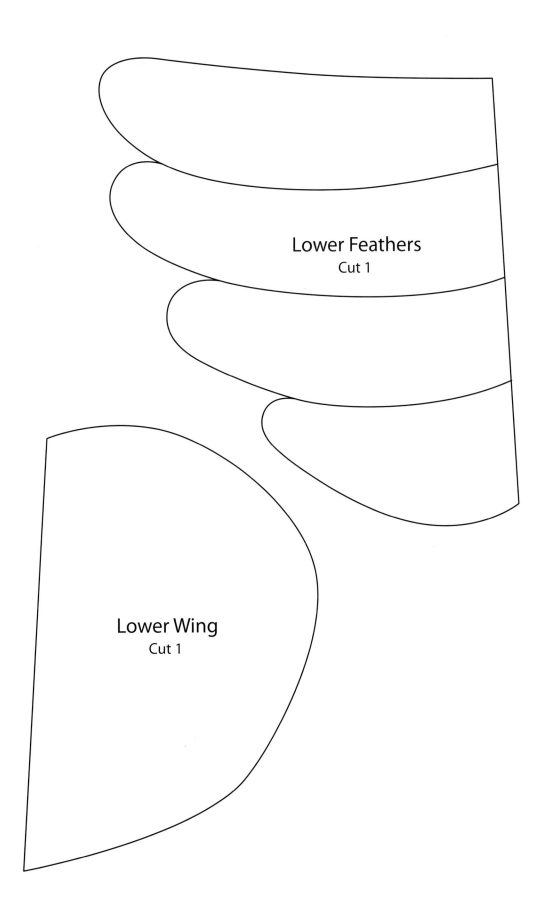

Lower Feathers
Cut 1

Lower Wing
Cut 1

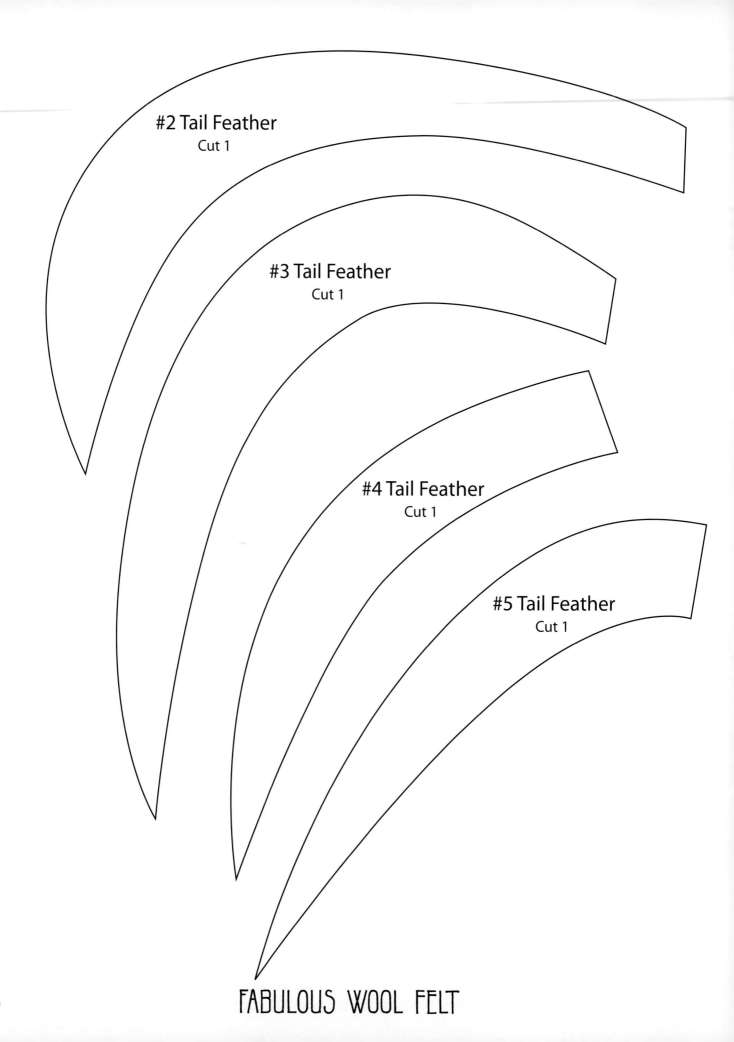

#2 Tail Feather
Cut 1

#3 Tail Feather
Cut 1

#4 Tail Feather
Cut 1

#5 Tail Feather
Cut 1

FABULOUS WOOL FELT

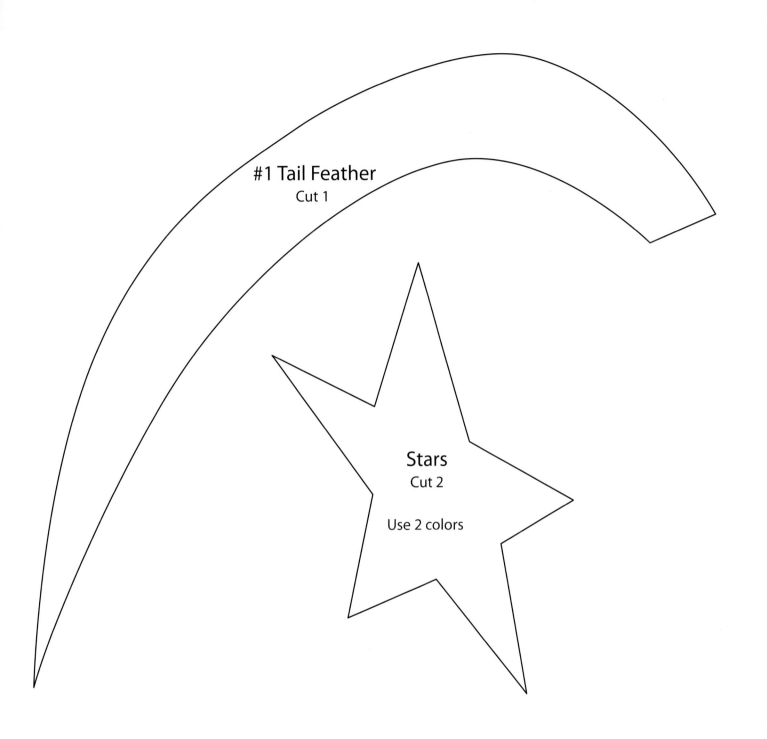

#1 Tail Feather
Cut 1

Stars
Cut 2

Use 2 colors

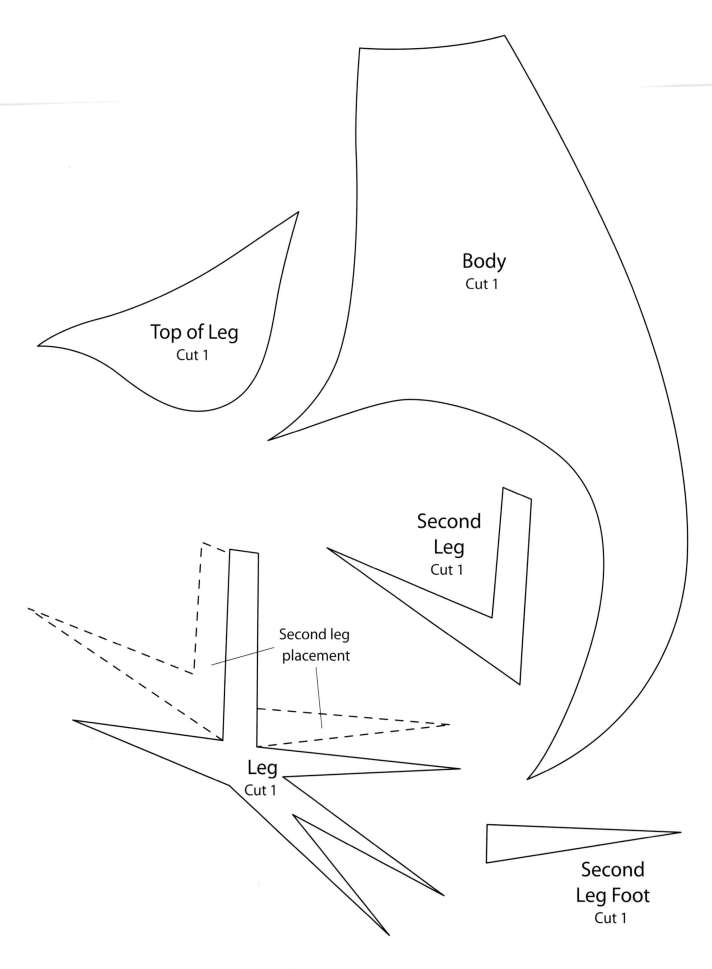

Body
Cut 1

Top of Leg
Cut 1

Second
Leg
Cut 1

Second leg
placement

Leg
Cut 1

Second
Leg Foot
Cut 1

FABULOUS WOOL FELT

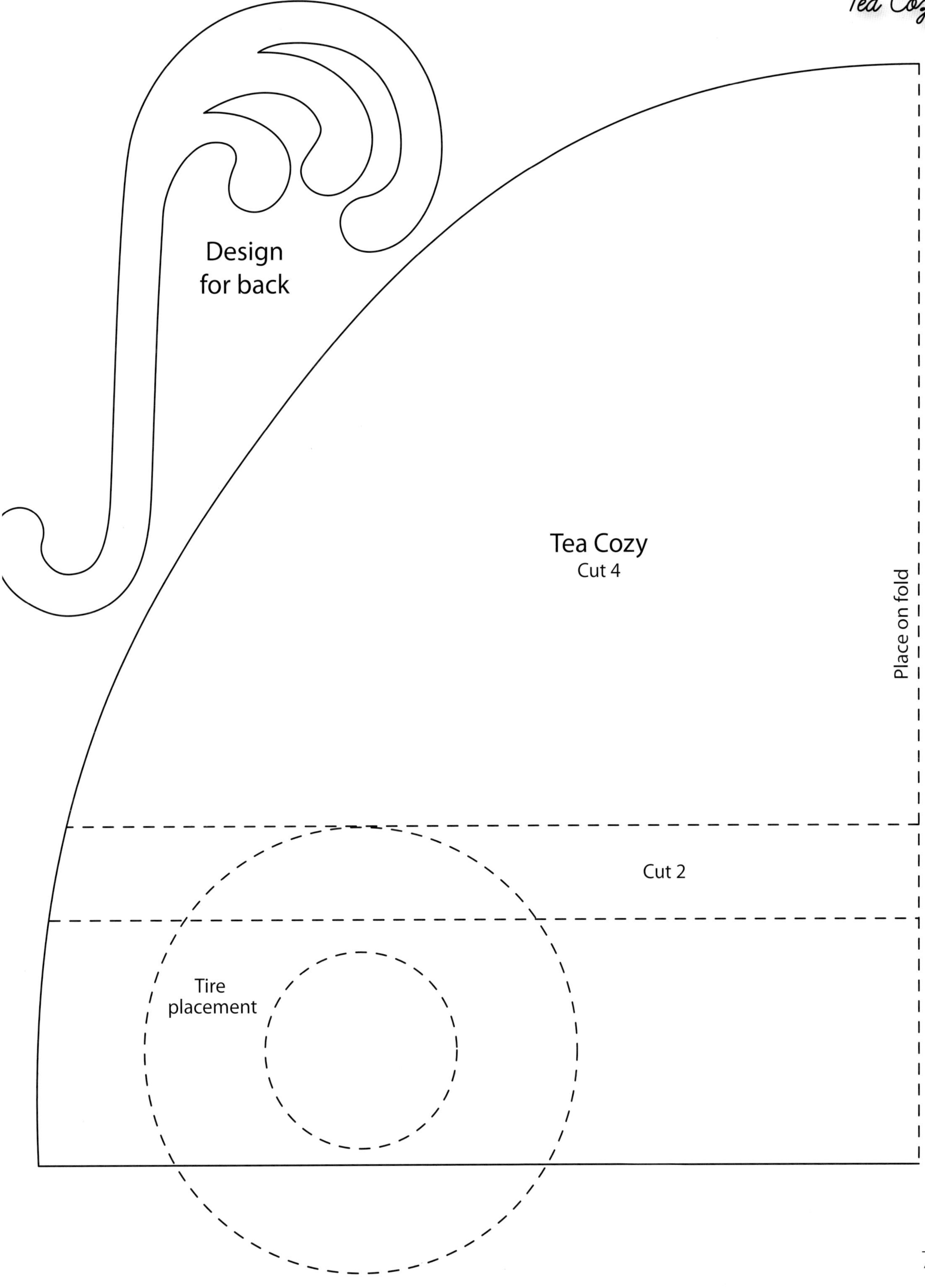

Design
for back

Tea Cozy
Cut 4

Place on fold

Cut 2

Tire
placement

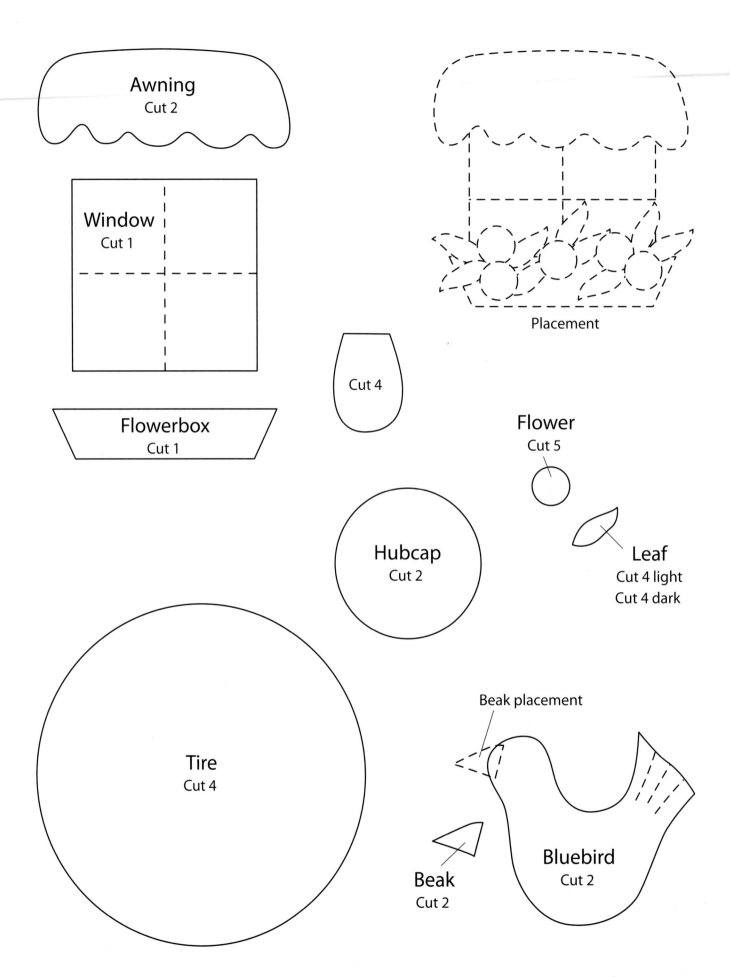

Awning
Cut 2

Placement

Window
Cut 1

Flowerbox
Cut 1

Cut 4

Flower
Cut 5

Leaf
Cut 4 light
Cut 4 dark

Hubcap
Cut 2

Tire
Cut 4

Beak placement

Beak
Cut 2

Bluebird
Cut 2

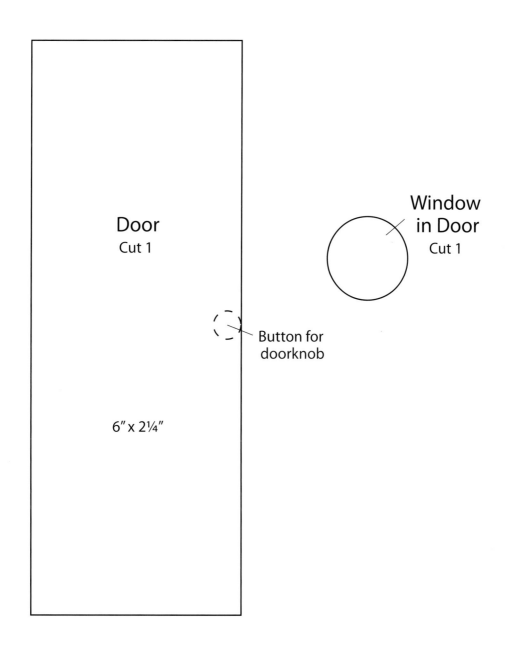

Door
Cut 1

6" x 2¼"

Window
in Door
Cut 1

Button for
doorknob

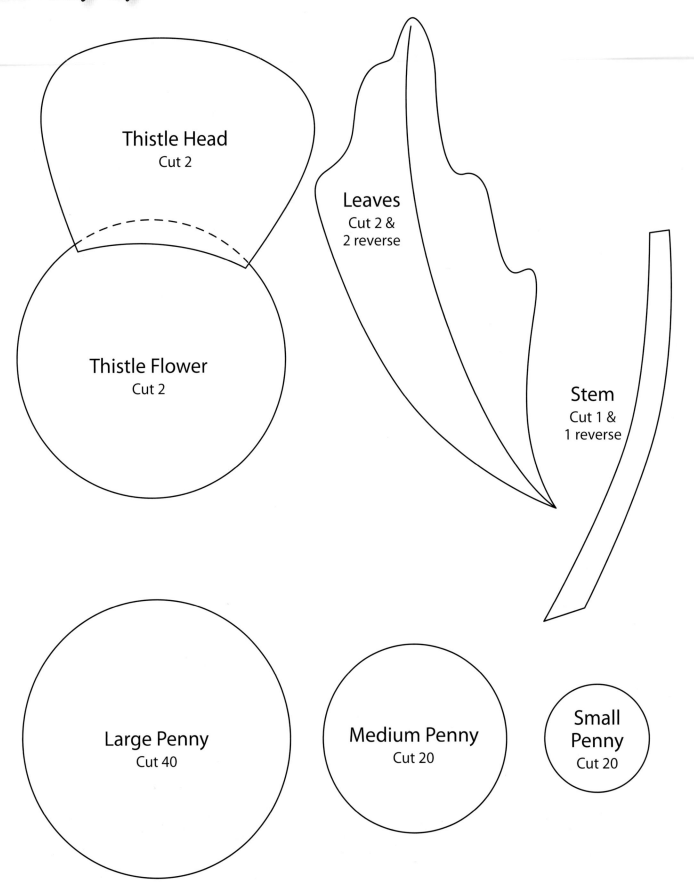

Thistle Head
Cut 2

Thistle Flower
Cut 2

Leaves
Cut 2 &
2 reverse

Stem
Cut 1 &
1 reverse

Large Penny
Cut 40

Medium Penny
Cut 20

Small
Penny
Cut 20

FABULOUS WOOL FELT

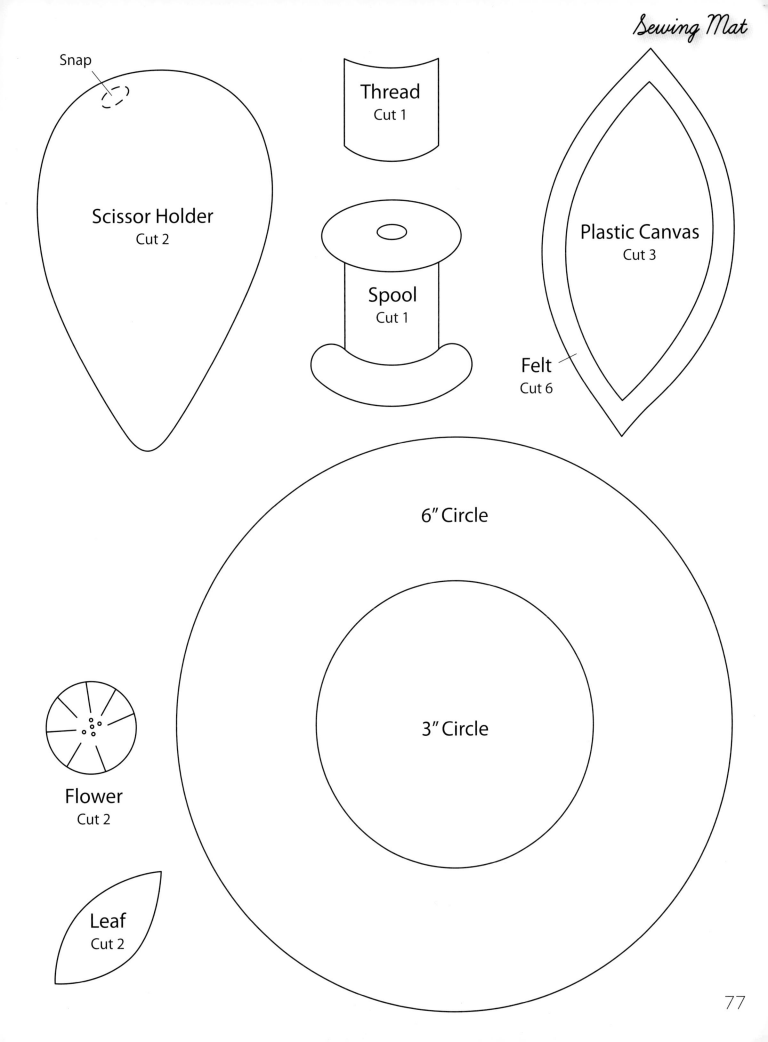

Snap

Scissor Holder
Cut 2

Thread
Cut 1

Spool
Cut 1

Plastic Canvas
Cut 3

Felt
Cut 6

6" Circle

3" Circle

Flower
Cut 2

Leaf
Cut 2

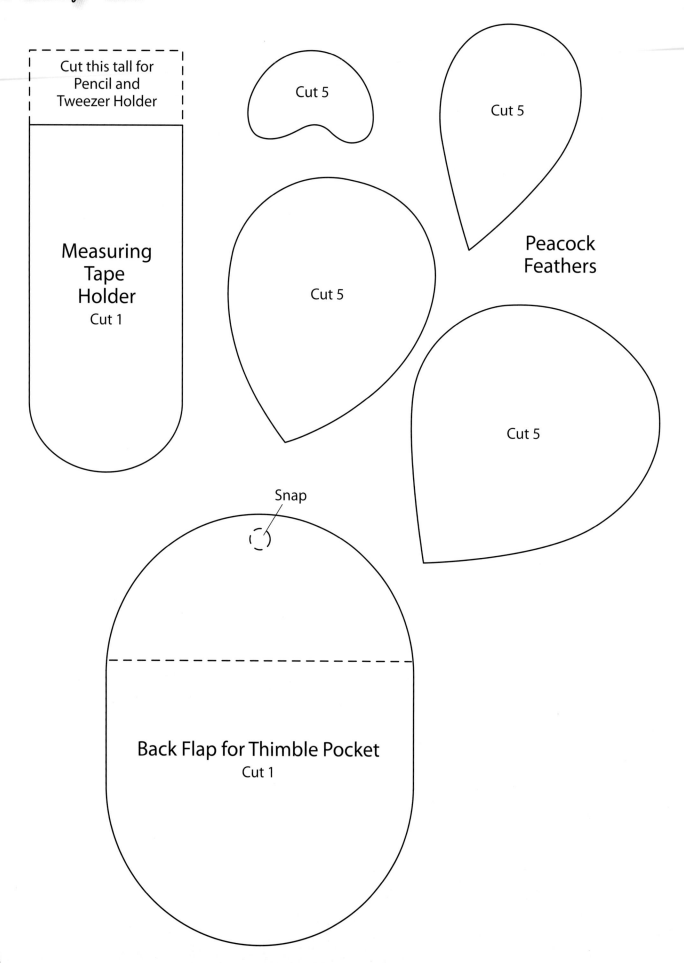

Cut this tall for
Pencil and
Tweezer Holder

Measuring
Tape
Holder
Cut 1

Cut 5

Cut 5

Peacock
Feathers

Cut 5

Cut 5

Snap

Back Flap for Thimble Pocket
Cut 1

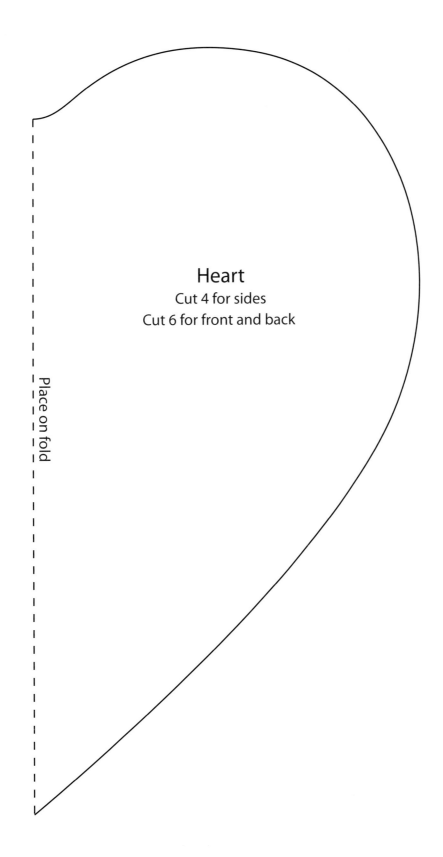

Heart
Cut 4 for sides
Cut 6 for front and back

Place on fold

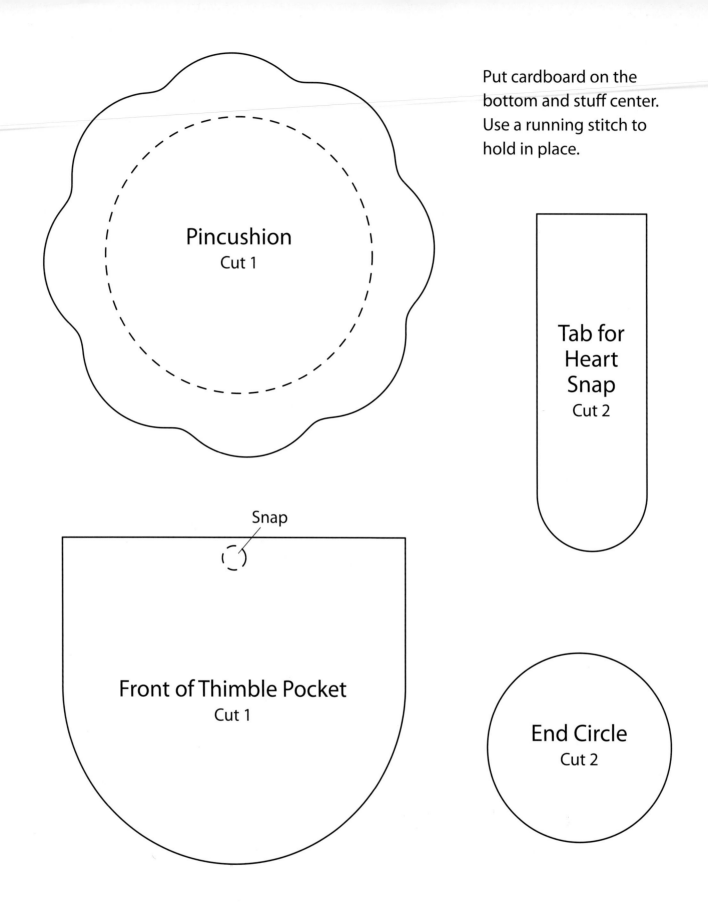

Pincushion
Cut 1

Put cardboard on the bottom and stuff center. Use a running stitch to hold in place.

Tab for Heart Snap
Cut 2

Snap

Front of Thimble Pocket
Cut 1

End Circle
Cut 2

FABULOUS WOOL FELT

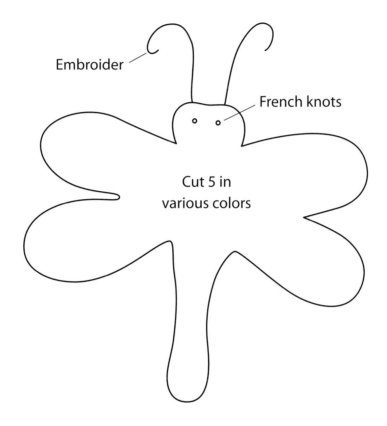

Embroider

French knots

Cut 5 in
various colors

Notes

Notes

Notes